STARTERS

Minibeasts

Lynn Huggins-Cooper

WAYLAND

Text copyright © Lynn Huggins-Cooper 2003

Consultant: Carol Ballard
Language consultant: Andrew Burrell
Design: Perry Tate Design

Published in Great Britain in 2003
by Hodder Wayland, an imprint of
Hodder Children's Books

This paperback edition published in 2007 by Wayland,
an imprint of Hachette Children's books

Reprinted in 2007

The publishers would like to thank the following for allowing us to reproduce their
pictures in this book: Papilio; cover, contents page 7, 9 (left), 17 / Corbis; 4, 18 (top)
Ralph A. Clevenger, 22, 24 (second from top) Ariel Skelley / Premaphotos Wildlife; 5
(bottom), 10 (top) Ken Preston-Mafham, 15 (bottom), 24 (fourth from top) Dr Rod
Preston-Mafham / Oxford Scientific Films; 6, 13 (bottom), 14, 15 (top), 16 (bottom),
19, 24 (bottom) / Heather Angel; 9 (right), 10 (bottom), 11, 18 (bottom), 21 (bottom),
24 (third from top) / NHPA; 12-13 (top) / Natural Visions; 16 (top) / Science Photo
Library; 20-21 (top), 23 / Getty; title page, 5 (top), 8, 24 (top)

A Catalogue record for this book is available from the British Library.

ISBN: 978 0 7502 4422 0

Printed and bound in China

Wayland
338 Euston Road, London NW1 3BH
Wayland is an Hachette Livre UK Company

Contents

Creeping, *flying,* swimming, LEAPING
– wherever you are, minibeasts are nearby.

Some minibeasts are insects. Insects always have six legs. If a minibeast does not have six legs, it is not an insect.

Ladybirds have six legs, so they are insects.

Stag beetles
have six legs, so
they are insects.

Spiders have eight legs,
so they are NOT insects.

Bug hunt

All over the world, gardens are full of wildlife. Minibeasts are SMALL, but they can be fierce hunters! These are predators.

Dragonflies catch flying insects. Their babies eat water insects, tadpoles – and even small fish!

Spiders eat flies and bugs. Sometimes, they catch them in their sticky webs.

A praying mantis sits very still, waiting for a bug to come along – and then it pounces!

Copy cats

Sometimes, minibeasts look like something else. They may be camouflaged, so they are the same colour as their surroundings.

Leaf insects look exactly like leaves!

8

Camouflage helps to keep minibeasts safe from predators – creatures that would eat them. It also helps them to hunt!

A flower mantis looks like a beautiful flower – until it pounces!

Stick insects look like dry old twigs.

All change!

Some baby minibeasts look just like their parents – but SMALLER!

Baby snails look the same as their parents.

Other minibeasts change as they grOW. They hatch from eggs and are called 'larvae'.

Caterpillars are baby butterflies and moths. They are 'larvae.'

They will go through a complete change before they become adults. We call this 'metamorphosis.'

This moth was once a caterpillar.

Monster minibeasts

Most minibeasts are quite small. But some are **HUGE**!

A dragonfly that lived at the same time as the dinosaurs had wings as **BIG** as a seagull!

Giant water bugs, found in America and Australia, can be as big as hamsters!

Queen Alexandra's birdwing butterfly is larger than many birds.

Giant African land snails can be as big as your hand!

Amazing minibeasts

Minibeasts can do amazing things!

A puss moth caterpillar has a fierce 'face' marking behind its head. It uses it to scare predators. This caterpillar can spit stinging liquid, too!

Dragonflies have special eyes that help them to see all round their heads.

Stink bugs put their bottoms in the air and squirt smelly liquid when they are scared – phew!

Master builders

Many minibeasts build homes for themselves.

Inside a hive or nest, bees make combs from wax. They store honey in the combs. It's where they keep their babies, too!

A caddisfly larva makes a case from pebbles, sticks, or even snail shells.

Termites build enormous mounds from sand, clay and spit. Sometimes they can be as tall as a house!

Helpful minibeasts

Some minibeasts are very helpful. Ladybirds and lacewings eat pests that harm plants.

Lacewings are the gardener's friend!

Earthworms help gardeners too. They travel through the soil making it rich and airy so plants will grow.

Other minibeasts like bees, make things that people can use.

Bees make sweet, yummy honey.

Harmful minibeasts

Some minibeasts are harmful because they have a poisonous bite, like black widow spiders.

When mosquitoes bite, they can make people very ill with diseases such as malaria.

Other minibeasts are harmful because they spread disease, damage crops or even buildings!

Woodworm burrow into wood and damage it.

Huge swarms of locusts eat and destroy crops growing in fields.

Be a minibeast explorer!

So minibeasts are found all over the world – even in your garden or park. Take a bug box, a magnifier and a camera, and explore!

Remember to be careful about touching minibeasts if there are poisonous bugs where you live! And always return them to their natural homes.

When you go outside, what will you find?

Glossary and index

Camouflage A way of disguising a creature to look like something else. **8-9**

Insects Creatures with six legs such as ladybirds, wasps, butterflies. **4-5**

Larvae Baby insects, which can often look like worms or maggots, are called larvae. **10**

Metamorphosis The change from a baby minibeast to an adult. **11**

Minibeasts Small creatures such as insects, worms and snails. Sometimes called 'bugs' or 'creepy crawlies'. **4-5**

Poisonous Something that causes death or harm. **20, 23**

Predator A hunter that catches and eats other creatures. **6, 9, 14**

Swarm A large group of flying insects. **21**